JUTLAND

SELIMA HILL

Jutland

BLODAXE BOOKS

ISBN: 978 1 78037 149 8

First published 2015 by
Bloodaxe Books Ltd,
Eastburn,
South Park,
Hexham,
Northumberland NE46 1BS.

www.bloodaxebooks.com
For further information about Bloodaxe titles
please visit our website and join our mailing list
or write to the above address for a catalogue.

Supported using public funding by
ARTS COUNCIL
ENGLAND

Cover design: Neil Astley & Pamela Robertson-Pearce.

Digital reprint of the 2015 Bloodaxe Books edition.

To my dear friend, Shipwreck;
also to Amy, whom I feel no need to impress.

ACKNOWLEDGEMENTS

Advice on Wearing Animal Prints was first published as a pamphlet by Flarestack Poets in 2009 and won the Michael Marks Poetry Award; some of the poems have since been revised. Thanks are due to *Poetry London* and *The Times Literary Supplement* where other poems have appeared. I would also like to thank the Centre for Hellenic Studies of Harvard University for their inspirational companionship and hospitality.

The epigraphs are from: Beat Sterchi: *Blösch* (The Cow), tr. Michael Hofmann (Faber, 1988); Slavoj Žižek: *The Sublime Object of Ideology* (Verso, 1989); Samuel Beckett: *Molloy*, tr. Patrick Bowles (Jupiter Books, 1955)

I would also like to thank Letty for the line 'Crocodiles that answer to their names'. And Sam Fairbrother for his list.

CONTENTS

Advice on Wearing Animal Prints

Sunday Afternoons at the Gravel-pits

Cows are made as if for standing still.

🙐 Beat Sterchi: *Blösch*

The effect of the real occurs in the joke about a patient who complains to his analyst that there is a big crocodile under his bed. The analyst explains to him that this is his paranoiac hallucination and gradually cures him, so the patient stops seeing him. A couple of months later, the analyst encounters on the street a friend of his ex-patient with the crocodile-idea and asks him how the patient is doing; the friend replies: 'Which one do you mean? The one who is now dead since he was eaten by a crocodile that was hiding under his bed?'

᠍ Slavoj Žižek: *The Sublime Object of Ideology*

I follow with my eyes the proud and futile wake.
Which, as it bears me from no fatherland away,
bears me onward to no shipwreck.

🙰 Samuel Beckett: *Molloy*

ADVICE ON WEARING
ANIMAL PRINTS

A

It's lying on the floor as good as gold.
It never moves. It never even cries.
It likes to simply lie there doing nothing.
But visitors complain it smells of stew.

B

No wonder it can't breathe – *it's bloody freezing!*
But how could someone do a thing like that?
Anyone could come in here and tread on it!
Could? They do! They kick it down the hall!

C

When Agatha arranges her unicorns
up and down the carpet in the dark,
somebody tells her she's an idiot –
but what she needs is a little hairdryer.

D

Agatha's a pretty little thing –
much *too* pretty, if you ask me!
She thinks she is entitled to have slaves
and pull their greasy tails till they mew.

E

Encumbered by her lace-encrusted dress,
she hurries down the street to the club.
The other girls are blonde and wear tutus.
Her bodice creaks as if it's made of floor-boards.

F

The older girls like bouncing on her face!
big horsey girls with faces like rosettes
who end another hot triumphant hack
by bursting in and bouncing on her face!
(She's only got one arm which is sad
but anyhow that's a good excuse
to do whatever she does *very slowly*.
I think she even *thinks* with one arm!)

G

She used to like blackcurrant juice and prayer
but now she lies in bed and likes nothing.
She thinks she is a child and she thinks
she's going to bleed to death but she isn't.

H

She smoothes and polishes the long hot hair
certain people say makes her beautiful
but certain people saying she is beautiful
is not a good idea in this case.
This person wants to kiss her but she bites him –
that's not the way to make new friends, Agatha! –
and Agatha is left on the floor,
her petticoats all crushed to death like piglets…
The unicorns are very small and cross.
They whinny in the dark for their groom.

I

When people pass the seat by the boating-lake
where Agatha is sucking on her pear
they wonder what she's thinking. She is thinking
she never wants to love someone again!
Suddenly two girls in red appear
and slide across the frozen lake like pistols
but Agatha prefers the little zoo
where often she's the only visitor.

J

Agatha likes sheep because sheep
aren't remotely interested in fun.
Nobody expects a sheep to party!
All they have to do is grow wool.

K

The weight of many things but mostly sorrow
weighs her down like meat in a sack.
She rolls against the door like a giant
who rolls against the door of a club
where giants in uncomfortable dresses
soothe each other with their large hands.

L

All afternoon her greasy yellow cat
hurls itself against the bedroom window.
Agatha can hear its yellow nails
squeaking on the glass between the flies.
It used to be such a sweet kitten!
Now it's bald and smells of fish and rubber.

M

She's on the terrace, dressed as a cow
(with real milk!) when a tall giraffe
bespangled with white fairy-lights comes up
and kicks her in the udder with its hoof
then totters off into the music room,
twinkling its electric tiara.

N

I'm sorry but she's so bad-tempered-looking
you'd have to be a saint to befriend her!
Well, luckily, some people are saints,
some people do befriend her – or they try,
but nobody befriends her satisfactorily
and so she soldiers on on her own.

O

She thinks a rat comes in and chews her nose
but Agatha, *there are no rats!* (And anyway
they'd never be attracted to *your* nose…)

P

Agatha has taken up jogging!
She does it *very slowly*. (One-armed joggers
should never really jog too fast, should they?)
Her underwear now comes in special boxes.
And every little nook is smeared with goose-fat.

Q

Yes, all they have to do – sheep I mean –
is not go wandering off on their own.
Agatha herself is good as gold
and rarely strays from her small flat.

R

It's like a lady's hand-bag it's so small –
but that's OK, she's only got one arm!
(That was mean. I'm sorry. I should say
how neat she is, and that her needs are *modest*.)

S

It's true she bites.
She bit a doctor once
who had to have eight stitches in his cheek!
(There's still a nasty scar and no one knows
he didn't get it *surfing in Hawaii!*)

T

Snow begins to fall and the sheep
walks away without looking back...
In her flat meanwhile sequinned slippers
are waiting like sharp tools to cause her pain.

U

They told her not to *time and time again*
but here she is, on the actual day,
walking down the aisle wearing animal prints!

V

While Agatha is hiding in the shrubbery
with one of her excruciating headaches,
a man in Cuban heels staggers past
then sinks against the holly with a curse.

W

She drags the piano through the open door
and out onto the terrace where she smashes it
and hurls the broken pieces at the dark –
then silence reigns and she falls asleep...

X

She sees an arm lying in the grass
and then a man runs across the field
shouting something Agatha can't hear
above the pounding of his huge trainers.

Y

She thinks he's going to kick her – and he is,
he's going to kick her now – can you believe that?
he kicks her with a foot like a Jutland's
(except the mighty Jutland's foot is feathered).

Z

They hear her gnawing at the skirting-board
but by the time they reach her
it's too late.
She's lying on the floor as good as gold.
No wonder she can't breathe: she's got no breath.

SUNDAY AFTERNOONS
AT THE GRAVEL-PITS

Mother may I go and bathe?

Yes, my darling daughter.

Hang your clothes on yonder tree

But don't go near the water.

  Traditional

Golfer in the Snow

My father, when he sees his new-born daughter,
stiffens like a golfer in the snow

who thinks he's going to cry when it hits him
he hasn't got a golf-course anymore.

The Lark

When he moves he moves as imperceptibly
as someone made of powdered cocaine,

his mouth against my skin like a lark
that's fallen from the sky and can't breathe.

My Father's Traps

My father likes to crush the necks of mice
in various traps he sets around the house,

mostly in the kitchen, where my mother
is candying her candied orange-peel.

Snowball

A snowball that's as big as a cherry tree
is pressing its white face against the window-pane

as if it's mine and wants to mother me
so even my own father will not know me.

Home

Home is somewhere cosy where it's cosy
and hamsters wouldn't dream of being dead,

where micturation doesn't pinch like earwigs
and daughters are a joy to be with.

My Stiff Organza

The body underneath my stiff organza
quivers like a body made of snails

that live apart inside a snail city
that's not so much a city as an aerodrome

where nothing can survive except snails
that thrive on boredom, secrets and tranquillity

and being left alone to crawl about
on runways where all traffic is forbidden.

When Everybody Else Is Asleep

When everybody else is asleep
my father is awake and what he does

he always does alone and smartly-dressed
the way a wolf is smartly-dressed in stories.

My Father's Knees

The embers flicker softly as I stand,
beside myself with rage, between the knees

that grip me like the guards of a palace
inhabited by moths made of gold-dust.

My Father's Beard

I know I never see him with a beard
but that's because he only puts it on

afterwards, when he's left the house
to go and live his other life, as God.

Cupboard

He's standing by my bed like a cupboard
standing with no face in the dark

but if I start to walk I think the cupboard
will suddenly start to walk too.

My Father with a Bowl of Peas

He sits her on his wrist and feeds her peas
as green as the canary is yellow,

unaware of being watched by someone
who should have been in bed hours ago.

My Father's Tin

The sugared almonds in the silver tin
are only there for children who are good,

and those like me who aren't can only watch
and picture in our dreams the birds who laid them.

Rubber

His lap is like a lap made of rubber
from which it isn't easy to escape

because this rubber is the sort of rubber
that makes your skin go red if it touches it.

Eileen

I don't know if he tries to help me love him
but if he does he fails, as he fails

to help me understand it isn't true
that nothing is worth loving but my rabbit.

The Doctor

The Doctor is the man I call The Doctor
who creeps around the house like a snail

creeping round the house on a foot
capable of everything but sound.

My Father's Chair

I never go towards it. On the contrary
I back away and then a firm hand

guides me from behind until I'm held,
beside myself with rage, between the knees

that grip me like a pair of sliding doors
nobody can open but the opener.

Dolphinaria

Normal dolphins love being dolphins;
normal artists give up chess for art;

normal icebergs calve without compunction
and normal fathers love their little girls.

My Father's Hands

Like gold and silver mice that smell of hyacinths
in darkened rooms, like wingless lorikeets,

his hands advance as if he isn't true,
as if he can't do wrong, like the Pope.

Rectitude

Everyone appreciates rectitude;
the smell of bridesmaids; freshly-driven snow;

the simple acts of little girls that glimmer
like pearls on necklines on behalf of oysters.

My Father Listening to Liszt on His Gramophone

Ever since I saw my father cry
I myself have refused to cry

even on the day I bury Eileen,
her body like a handful of meringues.

My Father as a Lorry

If a large refrigerated lorry
were made of sunshine, all my little friends

would marvel at it as they would at him
if my father were to speak to them.

God's Love

The savage-looking girls with scrunched-up hair
who thunder past my window on their bays

are throwing back their heads as if to say
they couldn't give a toss about His love for them.

My Father's Canary

She takes no notice of the little bell
(or something in the shape of a bell

that never tinkles), nor the cuttlefish,
nor the door I kindly prop open.

My Father's Suit

Even on a day like today,
my father always likes to wear his suit

and never lets the sun touch his body,
like kings and queens, who never do either.

No one Is Allowed

No one is allowed to come near me
and I refuse to love anybody

unless *I really want to* – and I know
I do not *really want to* love him.

French Poodle

When I get the chance to play French Poodle
I play it all day long like a maniac

until the cattle turn and walk away
as if to see how bored they can look.

The Wood at Midnight

He takes me to the middle of the wood
and leaves me there to come back on my own –

but it's not him but me who is triumphant
when morning comes and I'm still not home.

Disobedience

Ugly buildings should not be allowed;
he never sees a child without flinching;

my face is like the face of a shoebill,
and disobedience is disobedience.

The Correctly-inflated Airbed

The airbed is correctly inflated
but as he still insists on despising it

I take it to the river in the dark
before he is awake and float at dawn

when nothing is allowed except floating
and airbeds will make way for airless lily-pads.

My Father's Feet

My father's very proud of his body
and, most of all, of the tiny feet

he powders every afternoon like poodles
whose whiteness must be whiter than *Swan Lake*.

Who I Really Am

I know there's no such thing as who I am,
as someone knowing 'who I really am';

all I know is this: here's a man
who never taught his daughter how to whistle.

Sack-race

I'm hating every minute and the sun
never stops blinding me when suddenly

I'm being sick and as I'm being sick
I give up trying to please him altogether.

My Father's Horse

I should have been a girl he could have raped,
I should have been a woman, or a horse,

I should have been his own private swimming pool
but can't he see I'm not and I refuse to be.

Omnipotence

My father is omnipotent, we know that,
and he can do anything he wants;

anything, that is, except one thing,
that I can do easily: sin.

The Gravel-pits

Never trust a girl who hates her father;
never trust a girl who can swim;

never go alone to the gravel-pits
with somebody with arms and legs like rubble-crushers.

Men in Swimming-trunks on River-banks

Every night to get myself to sleep
I line up men in swimming-trunks on river-banks

and count them as they push each other in
but none of them is him or anything like him.

The Savage Girls with Shimmering Hair Who Jump

The savage girls with shimmering hair who jump
so close to where the rocks are I can't look,

who know that love is pointless, need to know
that if they think I love him they're mistaken.

Thickly-frozen Lakes

Like blocks of ice on thickly-frozen lakes
creaking as they re-adjust themselves,

my father can be heard behind the door
adjusting to my presence in the bathroom.

My Father's Crocodiles

Not only does my father not breed crocodiles
whose names and personalities are legendary

but also he refuses to acknowledge
that no one is as lovable as I am.

The Rock-hard Body of My Father's Daughter

The rock-hard body of my father's daughter
belongs to me, and no one else but me,

and nobody can stop me uprooting it,
walking it alone to the gravel-pits,

squeezing it inside a skintight swimsuit
and shaving off, and plucking off, its hairs.

My Father's Love

My father thinks he loves me but he doesn't,
or not enough, or in the wrong way,

and God Himself has told me, in confidence,
it's *just a waste of everybody's time.*

Visitor

My father has emerged from his study
and walks across the hall to the door

through which the silhouette can be seen
of somebody resembling the policewoman

for whom two chairs have been arranged upstairs
where she and I will come to our agreement,

assisted by the faint smell of petrol
with undertones of lily-of-the-valley.

Of All the Violent Girls at the Gravel-pits

Of all the violent girls at the gravel-pits
I myself am the most violent,

or so my father thinks, but even he
has no idea how violent I am –

how cold the water, how high-pitched the scream,
how close the secret of Eternal Life.

The Phrase 'Reaching Out'

When I'm 'reaching out', or when I'm trying to,
I never really know what I'm doing,

I only know that nothing seems to happen
except the usual large and small planets

calmly rearranging the sea
and maybe that's a good thing, I don't know.

Crocodiles That Answer to Their Names

I thought my father was uniquely bad
but any father would have seemed as bad

to somebody who wanted only crocodiles
that swallow stones and answer to their names.

Wolverine

Shall I spell it wolverine or wolvereen?
And what are clegs? And can't he understand

I'm trying to love him but I don't know how?
And is it true forgiveness is forgiveness

only if the person first repents?
That kindness isn't kindness but self-sacrifice?

Questions, questions, questions – but the answers,
like Valentines, are never enough.

My Father's Swimming-trunks

Everybody knows he goes swimming
but nobody has seen him in the water

or even in the lane but I myself
have seen his swimming-trunks in the airing-cupboard.

My Father's Crochet-hook

The crochet-hook and the sliced lemon,
as bright as rockpools, used to frighten me

because the smell of crabmeat made his hands
smell of severed hands police might find.

Mahogany

Although the bodies of the violent girls
that throw themselves against the shimmering lakes

may look as hard and glossy as mahogany,
they're nowhere near as hard as you might think.

Rage

I was so enraged by how my father
hadn't got a clue who I was,

it never crossed my mind that I myself
neither knew nor cared who *he* might be.

Hope

I know that if I'm ever to forgive him
I have to give up hope – by which I mean

hope for an entirely different past
to supercede the past I must forgive him for.

Coleslaw

But what if being kind is exploitative,
redundant, ineffective and demeaning,

and basically out of date – like coleslaw,
dancefloors, swimsuits, rosebuds, souvenirs?

if kindness is a virtue that's a virtue
for losers only, as a sort of bribe,

a way of being morally triumphant,
or thinking that you are but you're not?

Daisies

Because it's hard for us to understand
the only thing we have is the present,

we stand in groups and bleat like little lambs
wondering what's happened to our daisies.

The Absence of Love

It's not the *absence* of love; on the contrary,
it is its possibility that maddens us;

that comes so close yet seems so far away;
that flickers with a light we are unworthy of.

Fear

The only thing worth living for is fear,
to fear the thing I fear, which is intimacy,

intimacy fear will defy:
I tell myself the answer is to fear.

My Father's Daughter

Although I didn't choose to be his daughter,
my father, in a way, did choose me –

not me exactly, but the other daughter
I should have been but turned out not to be.

My Father's Smile

He smiled with the smile of a man
undisturbed by love and its indignities

whom nothing can deflect from his path
of being perfect till the end of time.

Tongue

First of all I will forget the tongue,
and secondly I will forget the mouth;

and then I will forget the room itself
in which he would secrete me like a cheese.

My Father's Forehead

It doesn't seem to be my place to do that,
it doesn't seem to be respectful to him,

after all it would have been unheard of
for me to kiss him when he was alive;

for me to even think it might be possible
for tenderness to override pain.

Lilies in their Arms

It's taken me all this time to realise
that he could feel pain as well as me

but now it's much too late to have loved him,
if not too late to be consumed by shame,

consumed by shame while hiding from his acolytes
who dash about with lilies in their arms.

Although Of Course I Know He Isn't Here

When I flinch like that when someone touches me,
although of course I know he isn't here,

I sometimes think it seems as if he is –
and then I'll quickly think of something else! –

but yesterday, in that split second,
I felt my heart go out to him, I mean

only for a second, which is nothing,
but to me it was like everything:

I saw him, or I thought I saw him, shiver,
as if he were a pool or a whippet.

Footnotes

Marcel Duchamp, at the height of his fame, gave up art for chess (see 'Dolphinaria').

'French Poodle' is a kind of underwater 'British Bull-dog' – for confident swimmers only.

In 2010, a crocodile was found living in a bungalow in Kent.

The Jutland is a heavy draught horse from Denmark.

Selima Hill grew up in a family of painters on farms in England and Wales, and has lived in Dorset for the past 40 years. She won first prize in the Arvon/*Observer* International Poetry Competition with part of *The Accumulation of Small Acts of Kindness* (1989), one of several extended sequences in *Gloria: Selected Poems* (Bloodaxe Books, 2008). *Gloria* includes work from *Saying Hello at the Station* (1984), *My Darling Camel* (1988), *A Little Book of Meat* (1993), *Aeroplanes of the World* (1994), *Violet* (1997), *Bunny* (2001), *Portrait of My Lover as a Horse* (2002), *Lou-Lou* (2004) and *Red Roses* (2006). Her latest collections from Bloodaxe are *The Hat* (2008); *Fruitcake* (2009); *People Who Like Meatballs* (2012), shortlisted for both the Forward Poetry Prize and the Costa Poetry Award; *The Sparkling Jewel of Naturism* (2014); *Jutland* (2015), shortlisted for both the T.S. Eliot Prize and the Roehampton Poetry Prize; *The Magnitude of My Sublime Existence* (2016); *Splash Like Jesus* (2017); *I May Be Stupid But I'm Not That Stupid* (2019); and *Men Who Feed Pigeons* (2021), shortlisted for both the Forward Prize and T.S. Eliot Prize.

Violet was a Poetry Book Society Choice and was shortlisted for all three of the UK's major poetry prizes, the Forward Prize, T.S. Eliot Prize and Whitbread Poetry Award. *Bunny* won the Whitbread Poetry Award, was a Poetry Book Society Choice and was shortlisted for the T.S. Eliot Prize. *Lou-Lou* and *The Hat* were Poetry Book Society Recommendations, while *Jutland* was a Special Commendation. She was given a Cholmondeley Award in 1986 and a University of East Anglia Writing Fellowship in 1991, and was a Royal Literary Fund Fellow at the University of Exeter in 2003-06.

She has worked on several collaborations with artists including: *Parched Swallows* with choreographer Emily Claid; *Point of Entry* with sculptor Bill Woodrow; and *Trembling Hearts in the Bodies of Rocks* with performance artist Ilona Medved-Lost.

www.ingramcontent.com/pod-product-compliance
Lightning Source LLC
Jackson TN
JSHW081319130125
77033JS00011B/356

* 9 7 8 1 7 8 0 3 7 1 4 9 8 *